A Living Art
and other poems

David T. Shoemaker

Distinguished Airs
Claymont, Delaware

PUBLISHED BY
Distinguished Airs
PO Box 464
Claymont, Delaware 19703

Copyright © 2018 by David T. Shoemaker
Illustrations Copyright © 2018 by David T. Shoemaker

ISBN: 978-0-9984975-1-8
ISBN (ebook): 978-0-9984975-2-5

All rights reserved. No part of the contents of this book may be reproduced or transmitted in any form or by any means without the written permission of the publisher.

Interior Design: Danielle McPhail,
Sidhe na Daire Multimedia
www.sidhenadaire.com

Interior Art: David T. Shoemaker
Cover Art: David T. Shoemaker and Dave Alden Hutchison

Cover Design: Mike McPhail
www.mcp-concepts.com

Image Processing: Mike McPhail
www.mcp-concepts.com

For Mom,
Whose love and encouragement made this possible

Sue,
Who makes my world a wonder

And the six,
Whose friendship has carried me through the dark places:
Jeffey Bears, Nevets, CT, The Lady Raven,
The Blue Fantastic, and Yat

Contents

Illustrations 1
Acknowledgements 5
Foreword 7

Friends and Family
The Shoemaker Kennings 11
Captivity 14
Resignation Day 17
Marqod 19
Alone 22
Threnody 25
The Understudy 27
Monterey 1989 28
Elegy to a Distant Father 31
Message From My Father 32
Feeding the Hungry 35
When the Raven Smiles 37
For Dallas 39
A Different Light 40
JRM 43
For Sunny 45
Gifts Given and Received 48
Jehovah's Gift 51
MEMory 52
The Torchbearer 55

Historical
Preliterate 59
Q 61
The Five Burdens 63
In The Valley 66
The Discovery 69
Ode to a Grecian Potter 71
What Many Have Seen and Heard 75
Concerned Citizens 79
Difficult 83
A Living Art 87

A Living Art

The Collaborator 89
Demuth's Dove 93
Valentine Conundrum 94
W.W. 96
UVB-76, aka "The Buzzer" 99
The Saint 101
Sweet Sorrow 103

MYTH AND FOLKLORE
Stingy Jack 111
Creation 115
Rustam's Fire 119
The Wedding Guest 123
The Refugee Child 127
A Visit From Krampus 129
The Galleon 133

SEASONS
Nature 137
Januarius 138
Spring 141
Come Away 142
Mother's Night 144

MELANCHOLIA
Voices from the Abyss 149
Lebensmüde 153
3 a.m. 154
The Last Goodbye 155
Bardsong 159
Identity 160

ADVICE
A Ceasaries 165
Lessons from Master Fong 166
Uncle Peter's Philosophy 169
Friendship 170
Karma 171
Saying Goodbye to Honalee 174

About the Author 177

Illustrations

"The Shoemaker", based on *"A Sad Case Before The Bench", (1891)* by Thomas Protheroe
"Soft and Tame", based on a news photograph posted by AsiaWire
"General Winter", based on a news photo by TASS news service
"Lord of the Dance", based on a promotional photo released by Sony Pictures Korea for the film "Call Me By Your Name"
"Loneliness", based on a photograph by David T. Shoemaker
"Tussle", based on "A group of boys watch a playground fight", c. 1935, George Woodbine, Science Museum Group collection
"Taking the Stage", based on an photograph from "The Trans Man and the Theatre" by Bailey C.
"Coastal Highway 1" based on a photograph by *Great American Things*
"The Garf", based on a photograph by Jeffrey H. Shoemaker
"From the Bottom of the Stairs", based on a photograph by Joe Schmelzer
"The Vampyr", based on a still from "Nosferatu" (1922)
"The Raven", based on a photograph by Stephen C. Dickson
"PM II", based on a photograph by David T. Shoemaker
"JRM", based on a photograph by Paul P. Mouratedes
"Blanket and Painting" by David T. Shoemaker
"Ectoplasm", based on a photograph by Albert Freiherr von Schrenk-Notzing
"The Last Piece", based on a photograph by David T. Shoemaker
"The Torchbearer", based on *"Diogène", 1873, by* Jules Bastien-Lepage
"Qaqortoq Petroglyphs", based on a photograph by David T. Shoemaker
"CW Burial", based on a photograph BY JURAJ LIPTÁK
"Prenomen and Nomen", based on a photograph by David T. Shoemaker

A Living Art

"The Man in KV-62", based on a photograph by Harry Burton
"The Discovery", based on a photograph by Harry Burton
"Play On", based on an Attic Red Ware Lekythos in the Museum of Fine Arts, Boston
"King Xuan", based on a Ming Dynasty image of King Wen of Zhou
"Harlem River Club", based on a photograph of The Keyhole Club 1940s, photographer unknown
"Difficult Star", based on a photograph by David T. Shoemaker
"That was a moment" by David T. Shoemaker
"Collaborator", based on a photograph "Anschluss Tears" in the U.S. National Archives and Records Administration
"Soar", based on a photograph of Wilbur Wright taken October 10, 1902
"Demuth's Dove", based on a photograph by David T. Shoemaker
"Valentine", based on a Victorian Valentine Card
"The Saint", based on a photograph by David T. Shoemaker
"Little Mable", based on a Victorian Mourning Photograph, photographer unknown
"Jack O'Lanterns" based on a photograph by David T. Shoemaker
"Protos and Oudeteros" based on the photograph *"Children Playing Marbles, 1970," Manchester Daily Express*
"Rustam's Fire", based on a photograph by Doll Faced Persian Kittens
"The Captain", based on an illustration in *Male Character Costumes, a Guide to Gentlemen's Costume Suitable for Fancy Dress Balls and Private Theatricals*
"The Galleon", based on "The Flying Dutchman" (1900) by Howard Pyle
"Refugee Child" based on the painting *"Massacre of the Innocents" (1824) by Leon Cogniet*
"Krampus" based on a vintage Christmas card
"Resting from the Hike", photograph by David T. Shoemaker
"Januarius", based on an ancient sculpture of Janus
"Spring" based on a painting by Michael Cheval
"Come Away", based on the painting "The Storm" (1880) by Pierre Auguste Cot

David T. Shoemaker

"Shepherds hurple", based on a photograph from the Daily Mail
"Night Voices", based on a painting by Alex Grey
"Dying Light" based on an ad for ½ watt flashlight bulbs by superbrightleds.com
"Fog strangled alley", based on a photograph by Brassai
"Bardsong" based on the painting "Orpheus and Euridice" by Sergei Panasenko-Mikalkin
"Reflecting" based on the painting "Narcissus" by Caravaggio
"Little Boots", based on an ancient sculpture of Caligula
"Master Fong", based on a photograph of Sifu Francis Fong, photographer unknown
"A Day Off", based on the painting "Huckleberry Finn" by Worth Bream
"Karma", based on a photograph by David T. Shoemaker
"Square-rigged Brig" based on the painting "Brig Mercury after victory (1848) by Aivazovskiy

Acknowledgements

This chapbook is the culmination of a journey that began in the 5th grade, along a path from which I often strayed. I was guided back on the path in August, 2015, when I suggested a story idea to my friends Jake and Steve, and they challenged me to write it myself. Thanks for the nudge and encouragement.

Thanks to my Beta readers: Tim, Wolf, Greg, Hop, Marcella, Middle Dave and Clover—Your thoughtful criticisms and suggestions have improved these verses far more than I can say. Thank you for continuing to challenge me to defend my choices, tighten my meter, and clarify my vision.

I am grateful to the members and guests of the Newark Arts Alliance, the Arden Poetry Gild, Second Saturday Poets, and the Poetry Vortex for welcoming me into the fold and encouraging me to continue this journey, especially Maria, Greg, Bob, Dallas, Marty and Crucial.

Lastly, all my love and gratitude to my family, especially Sue, for their sacrifice of time together to allow me to pursue new avenues of creative expression. You have truly made my world a wonder!

Foreword

Over the three years, I have been presenting my poetry at various open mic events in New Castle County, Delaware. I have often been asked, "When's the book coming out?", to which I responded "When I have written enough poems that I am happy with."

You see, even though I have been writing poetry since the 5th Grade, I have not written consistently. Long periods of time would pass without writing anything, punctuated by brief—usually melancholy—periods of writing. This chapbook includes poems from three of these periods: the first dates to 1989-1991, when I was in college; the second to 2003-2006, after the deaths of my Father and Best Friend, and the third starting in August, 2015.

What sets this third period apart is that it was not in response to tragedy or depression. It started with a challenge: one night after book club, my friends Jake and Steve were discussing ideas for short stories. I had recently read about the rediscovery of the ancient Roman catacombs in 1578, and how the Pope, guided by the Holy Spirit, would point out the remains of various saints. The bones would then be cleaned and sent to churches in Northern Europe as part of the Counter Reformation. Today, most people believe they were ordinary Romans—not even Christians, let alone Saints! I was intrigued by the idea of a pagan spirit whose remains were taken to be a saint. What would he think of being "born again"? I suggested the idea to Jake and Steve, who both said I should write it myself. I demurred; I had tried writing short stories in college, without much success. I told them I might be able to do it as a poem instead, and they told me to go for it.

So, I went ahead and wrote "The Saint" and sent it to them. I don't think they thought I was serious (or capable) of writing the poem. Jake's response was "Uh Dave, that's absolutely brilliant.

A Living Art

Holy crap." They suggested I read it at the Newark Arts Alliance Open Mic Night, which started me on this odyssey and revived my interest in poetry.

I still find it difficult to write unless I am inspired. Usually, I will read something and hear a first line or phrase in my head. When that happens, the poem comes easily. As a result, most of my poems are based on stories from History or Folklore, rather than expressing beauty or emotions. In some ways, I feel more like a Bard than a Poet—though I have yet to set my verse to music...

In addition to writing poetry, I am also an avid photographer and fledgling painter. I decided to include some of my work as illustrations. I hope these pictures enhance your enjoyment and understanding of the poems.

Friends and Family

The Shoemaker Kennings

I am the Great Grandson
Of Howard Garfield Shoemaker
Of Chester, Pennsylvania,
The first of his name;
Husband of Lula,
Father of Rupert and Mary;
Tinkerer, mechanic,
Possessor of the Brownie Camera
And the Dark Room;
The Quiet One;
Drinker of Ketchup.

I am the Grandson of Rupert Francis,
Called Pop or Shupe;
Husband of Jeanette and Julia,
Father of Howard, Ronald, and Esther,
Stepfather of Gary and Priscilla;
Player of the Sax and the Clarinet,
Welder of Ships.
One Eyed like Odin,
Capturer of the Female Form,
Prankster.

I am the Son of Howard Garfield the Second,
Sometimes called "The Garf",
Number One Son;
Husband of Kay and May,
Father of David and Jeffrey;
The Lone Eagle,
Pilot of the Navion,
Builder of the Kingfisher and the Cubby,

A Living Art

Capeless Superman of River Ranch,
The Voice on the Airwaves,
November Three Delta Yankee Charlie,
Sharer of Jests and Cartoons,
Eater of Donuts,
Sunoco's Third Generation Shoemaker,
Shutterbug.

I am the Living Tribute to Beloved Thomas,
Husband of Suzan,
Brother of the Jeffey Bear;
Eaglet One,
The Historian Poet,
The Demuth Scholar,
Hatmaker to the 1st Continental Regiment of Foot,
The Crosser of Oceans,
Visitor to the Northern Lands,
The Russian Hawk,
The Bear Maker of New Castle,
MCFUD,
The Dapper One.

David T. Shoemaker

Captivity

How I long to be the Tiger of my Youth:
Fearless and hungry for life.
To some a terror I suppose
But to others,
Proud and Majestic.
I was lulled by the comforts of captivity;
I've become soft and tame.
Too long have I lain in the sun
Taking whatever food my keepers gave me
While opportunity slipped through my paws
like swift prey.
How I long to be the Tiger of my Youth!

David T. Shoemaker

A Living Art

Resignation Day

Today is my Resignation Day.
Today I will break the bonds that tie me to this life:
The endless grind of my job
With no future and no end;
To the house that's never clean;
To the bills which are never fully paid;
To the endless repetition of mornings and evenings
Which mark the passing of my days—
Each more similar to the one before
Until they blend into a seamless none.

I will then be free to search the world and go
Learn what I am to be before I'm cinder.
I will be free to photograph the falling flakes of snow
That cap the Kremlin's crenellated walls in winter.
I will be free to sift the shifting sands that blow
Across Saqqara's steps; the drifts which hinder
The ragged robbers from their wrongful plunder.
I will be free to dive into the darkened deep
To dance among Titanic's ferrous ghosts
I will be free to climb upon Tibetan peaks
To join the chanting of the Saffron host:
Perhaps before I'm done my heart will weep
For the memory of what I miss the most:
Your Love for me that made my world a wonder...

Your Love draws me back to this simple life
Unremarkable, but real.
The shared jokes and laughter,
Saying the same words at the same time,
The warmth and comfort of your embrace.

A Living Art

But even more than these everyday joys, it's
Knowing that I am not alone in the world
Because there's another person just like me.
Today is my Resignation Day
But the only thing I'm resigning is myself
To an ordinary life—made extraordinary by you.

Marqod

An aging theater has been revived
A place to go to feel alive
The marble stairs and chandeliers
Have come from far away Algiers
The Persian rugs have been replaced
New wallpaper in perfect taste
The Orchestra seats have been removed
The lighting and sound have been improved
On the stage, a band is playing
While below the crowd stands swaying
Above them all I sit enthroned
In the balcony, all alone
The music has a festive beat
The crowd begins to move their feet
When at the back I chanced to see
A young man dancing merrily
He had no partner, he didn't care
What others thought or if they stare
The music held him in its spell
Joy flowed from him as from a well
Even from my distant seat
I could feel the elation in his feet
I watched like Israfel's giddy stars
As he danced along to the music's bars
I wished that I could join with him—
To feel the joy he felt within
But my life's more the shadow kind
To grief my heart is more aligned
So, though I see the shining Joy
Radiate from the dancing boy
It's an emotion beyond my grasp

A Living Art

A fervor that I cannot clasp
Instead I wear a cheerful face
To move among the human race
So others never see the depth
Of my grief, nor how bereft
Are the passing of my days
In this anhedonic haze.
I marvel at this simple boy
Suffused with an unbridled joy
And wish, just once, that I could be
Riant, Joyful, and Free as he.

David T. Shoemaker

Alone

From Childhood's hour, I have not been
As others were—I have not seen
As others saw—I could not bring
My passion from a common spring.
From the same source I have not taken
My Sorrow; I could not awaken
My heart to joy at the same tone
And all I lov'd, I lov'd alone.
Then—in my childhood—in the dawn
Of a most disjunct life—was drawn
To a form that looked the same:
A Twin known by another name.
He too saw not as others saw,
From the well, no joy could draw.
Alone, he sat against the wall
While other boys played with a ball.
I looked, and saw myself in him;
I sat beside him on a whim.
My fate was changed, he did respond:
We talked, and smiled, and formed a bond
That made our lives forever better—
For now we lov'd alone, together.

© January 15, 2018 Edgar A. Poe and David T. Shoemaker

David T. Shoemaker

A Living Art

Threnody

What has kept us so long apart
When once we were so close?
What words I spoke cut to your heart
What wounded you the most?
I know the blame is mine to bear
For the verbal fight we fought.
A crimson stain of shame I wear
Each time I give it thought.
I know you tried to walk away
Before it was too late—
I should have let you go that day
But my anger was too great.
My anger blinded me to all
The joy I was to lose,
The comfort that a single call
Could summon for my use.
I threw away our friendship
With some petty, spiteful words
But worse was never giving lip
To the words you should have heard.
And now it is too late to mend
The bond we used to share;
The apology I long to send
Finds only empty air.
A mound of freshly cycled earth
Is all that's left to find
Of my brother given not by birth
But of a love we shared in kind.

A Living Art

The Understudy

There was no announcement from the stage,
No note in the program.
But the star was called away tonight
So now I must perform.
It is a tricky role to play—
Well known and loved by all.
The bone dry quips have a sharp edge
That must float and lightly fall.
Play it broad for an easy gag
And the laughter will ring false;
Too quiet and retiring
And the role will lack a pulse.
I step on stage with a heavy heart,
For I know the role's not mine,
And do my best to make them forget
The star no longer shines.
The scene is done, the lovers wed,
And no one shed a tear
For the Uncle who could not be there;
My gift to friends so dear.

Monterey, 1989

Along the coastal highway
Between the mountain and the sea
My Father practiced driving
And photography.
One side a wall of granite
One side a Nestea plunge
No hands on the steering wheel
I wonder how it's done.
One hand on the shutter
One hand on the lens
Both knees on the steering wheel
To drive around the bends.
Other people stop their cars
At scenic overlooks
To take the pictures that they put
In their memory books.
My Father's not the kind of man
To settle for such views;
He'd rather risk a bumpy ride
To capture rainbow hues.

David T. Shoemaker

A Living Art

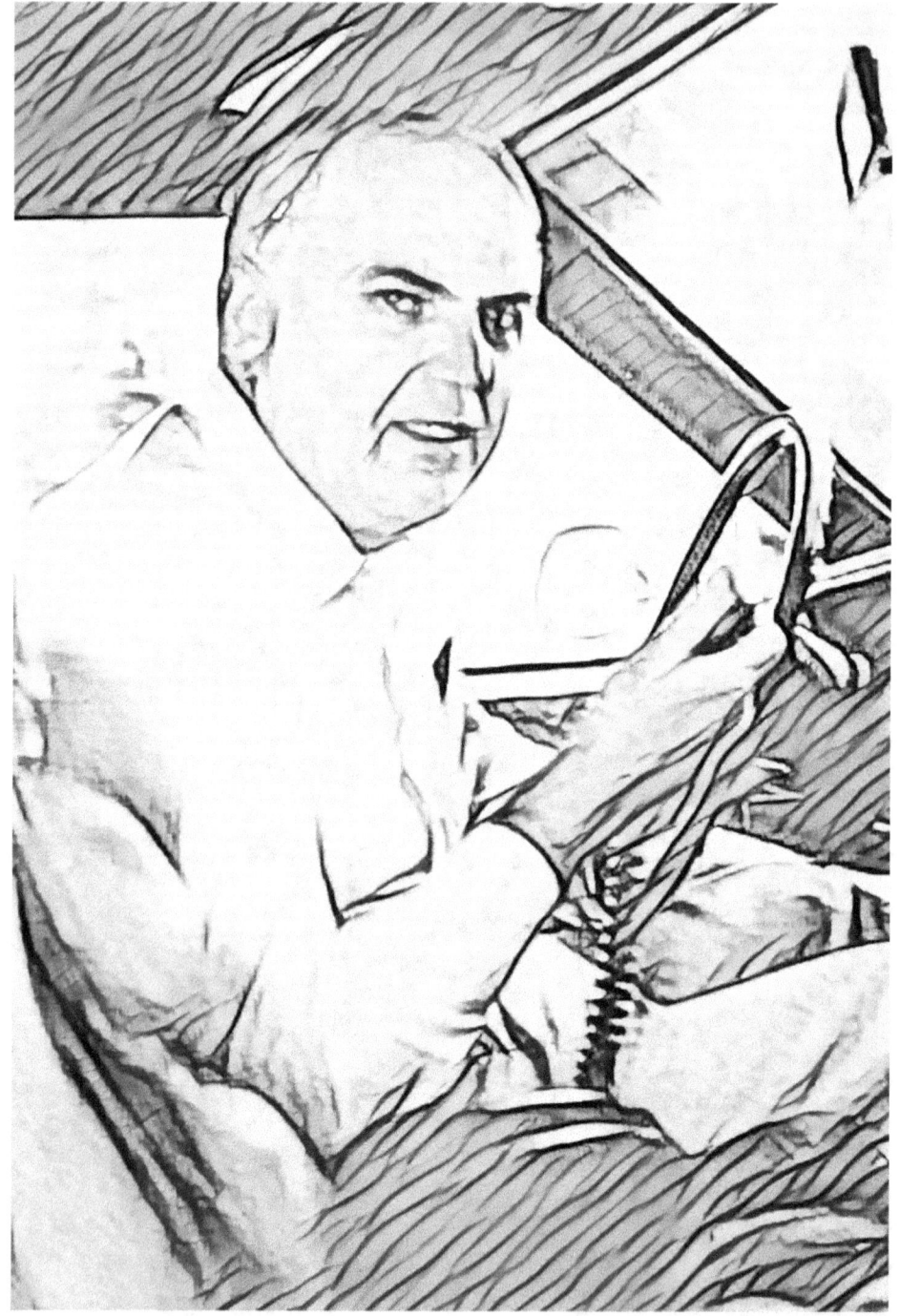

Elegy to a Distant Father

Who is, or was, my Father
Now that he is gone?
A distant seed long planted,
An echo in a song?
A smiling face in photos
Though never one at home.
He'd brag about me to his friends
But yell at me alone.
A bald man hiding from the world
Beneath three strands of hair.
For all it seems you've given me
Why should I even care?
And yet I feel so empty
Now that you are gone.
I wish we'd had a better life
Before your time was done.

Message from My Father

He called to me once,
As if from far away.

Dad called my name
Like he used to do
When I was a child
Sitting in my room—
Lost in a book—
As dinner grew cold on the table.

He said my name twice
As he often did
From the bottom of the stairs:
Softly at first,
Barely registering,
Then louder, insistent,
Demanding a response.

He called me once
As if from far away,
But I knew he was already gone.

David T. Shoemaker

A Living Art

Feeding the Hungry

I went to see the vampires,
Imagine my dismay
When they took one look upon me
And sent me on my way.

They looked me up and looked me down
Then consulted with each other.
One turned to me and with a frown
Said "No thanks, we'll find another".

I could tell that they were hungry
And should really have a bite
But I guess my blood's a little off—
Does it sour overnight?

Does this mean I'll soon join them
On the other side of Life?
Am I nearing my own end?
Should I notify my Wife?

Perhaps I'll call the digger
With his shovel and his pick—
Or maybe my spaghetti
Had way too much garlic.

A Living Art

When the Raven Smiles

The Raven is a brooding bird
With Sable feathered locks
Who seldom utters any word
And avoids the larger flocks.
He carries on in silence
Without giving any sign
Of his own life's jubilance
Or the joy he's brought to mine.

But I know I'm blessed and gifted
To have seen his visage shifted
And my shrouded soul is lifted
When the Raven Smiles.

The Raven is a noble bird
With a deeply caring heart.
Who feels the pain you're suffering
And tries to take his part.
He won't speak words of comfort
Just enfolds you in his wings;
And the sympathy within his eyes
Erases darker things.

But when my life has drifted
And my heart is rent and rifted
Every doubt and fear is lifted
When the Raven Smiles.

The Raven's not a flightless bird—
A thought that gives me pause—
And he can leave a deeper wound

A Living Art

Than those caused by his claws.
His absence leaves a gaping hole
Within my beating heart;
A longing for a treasure
Not found on a pirate's chart.

Then my life is bleaker,
My confidence is weaker;
I become a desperate seeker
Of the Raven's smiles.

For Dallas

Red, Green, Stop, Go;
Doors may open, Doors may close.
Many stops along the way—
I cannot rest, I cannot stay.
As we drive our route in Life
We may encounter bumps and strife.
People join us for a while;
It may be years or just a mile.
All are parted in the end—
If we are lucky, we gain a friend.
Opportunities pass like closing doors,
But this is not cause for remorse—
Another bus will soon come by
With welcoming doors opened wide!
Red, Green, Stop, Go;
Doors will open, Doors will close.
Many stops along the way;
I will not rest, I will not stay.

A Different Light

When I looked at you,
I saw Joey Ramone
And Marilyn Manson,
Poe's Raven
Or Rice's Lestat.
I saw the Black Stallion
And the Lord of Illusions.
I saw everything
Except the sad young man
Mourning for the woman
You longed to be.

David T. Shoemaker

A Living Art

JRM

You changed your clothes
And started down a new path.
You gave up the funereal black
And melancholy shades
Of purple and green,
The darkness left you,
And light poured forth
In pink and white.

You changed your name
And began your transformation.
Where once you had been
"Small" and "Humble",
The second of your name,
Now you were increased—
If not by Jehovah,
Then by the Goddess you adored.

You changed your smile
That first drew me to you.
Your shy, dimpled, tight lipped grin,
Full of mirth and mischief,
Yet contained and quiet.
That smirk is gone,
But in its place
A joyous, radiant, toothsome smile—
Broad,
Confident,
And full of peace.

What else would you have changed

A Living Art

If you had the time?
Would you have learned French
As you often said you would?
Would you have travelled?
Perhaps. But I suspect
You would have rather spent your time
Helping others on this path
To discover who they truly are,
As you had struggled to do.
And maybe more importantly,
You would have taught those
Not on your path
The true meaning of empathy.

For Sunny

Death is not governed by breaths and heartbeats
These signs can deceive:
For death is governed by the soul
And can affect those who still breathe.
This I know and I tell true
Because I was dead 'til I met you.

From dawn to dusk I moved about
Hoping none could tell
That every action was a habit;
That this world was my hell.
But all of that was at an end
When I met you and was your friend.

But I was young and didn't know
the treasure that I had.
When times were tough I ran and hid;
I never dreamed the love we had
was stronger than the force of atoms splitting—
that it would outlast the sins I was committing.

For two years now I thought that it was over
that the idea of us was better than reality.
I've tried to replace you half a dozen times;
But when I looked at them, your face I'd see.
And it's the ease that haunts me like a ghost
with which I threw away all of our hopes.

I must not have a brain that's worth a damn
to have walked away from you without a fight.
The times I spent with you were more than bliss

A Living Art

more than perfection, brighter than Heaven's light
To get you back I would give all I had or would ever earn
and all my children's wealth for a hundred generations
yet unborn.

Your smile fills my heart with hope,
Your laughter brings me light
To chase away the shadows
That shroud my heart at night.
All this and more you've done for me
By sharing who you are with me.

I know that what I've done to you
deserves no second chance.
For the suffering I've put you through
I don't deserve a second glance.
So if the thought of me brings you nothing more than
pain,
I will sadly step aside and hope happiness you gain.
For the loss of my true love I've only myself to blame.
But if there is a God and He shines His face on me,
My love for you will flood your heart and wash away the
pain.
It will lift away the hurt you feel, float it like a boat
Nothing dark will be left behind—gone will be every stain.
We may still have a chance to start anew
And this time to my word I will be true.

Though I'd love to give you diamonds
to make you richer than the Romanovs.
I'd love to give you a Castle in the Air
or an island with a sign "KEEP OFF!"
where we could spend our lives in peaceful bliss.
But I do not deserve a dream like this.

Instead I offer you just a small cottage
built beside a steady flowing stream.
Its rooms would all be small and very cozy

David T. Shoemaker

its ceilings low and with exposed beams.
Its living room would have a sunny spot
where we could sit and feel the gentle breeze
and hold each other close, or read, or watch
as our children played in our garden on bended knees.
It would not matter where I went to work
with such a home to come to I would be
richer than an oil soaked sultan
and happier than the Windsors seem to be.

This is my offer and my hope as well;
it is not much, yet more than I can tell.
You are the answer to my every question—
You and You Alone my wants can quell.
You are my heartbeat and my every breath
Without you I will resume my death.

Gifts given and received

You asked me not to give you more
You owe me too much now.
But the things I gave seem trivial
Compared to the gifts that you endow.
A story, a blanket, a bag of rolls,
A painting that's a decade old,
A blender with a broken lid—
You act as if they're solid gold.
You pushed yourself to collapse
To hold me straight and tall,
And held me tight within your arms
So that I wouldn't fall.
You welcomed me with open arms
When I felt out of place.
Your smile fills my soul with light
My grief it can displace.
You let me see what might have been
And do what couldn't be done.
If either of us owes a debt,
Surely, I am the one!
But gifts are not gifts with strings attached
And obligations to be met.
They must be given with an open heart
And no hope of things to get.
Perhaps that's why the ancients said
"Friends hold all things in common".
There would be no sense of debt or loss
To bring strife among the Brahmin.
So from today, what's mine is yours;
Take anything you need:
My Time, My Wealth, My Goods, My Love;
From your shackles you are freed!

David T. Shoemaker

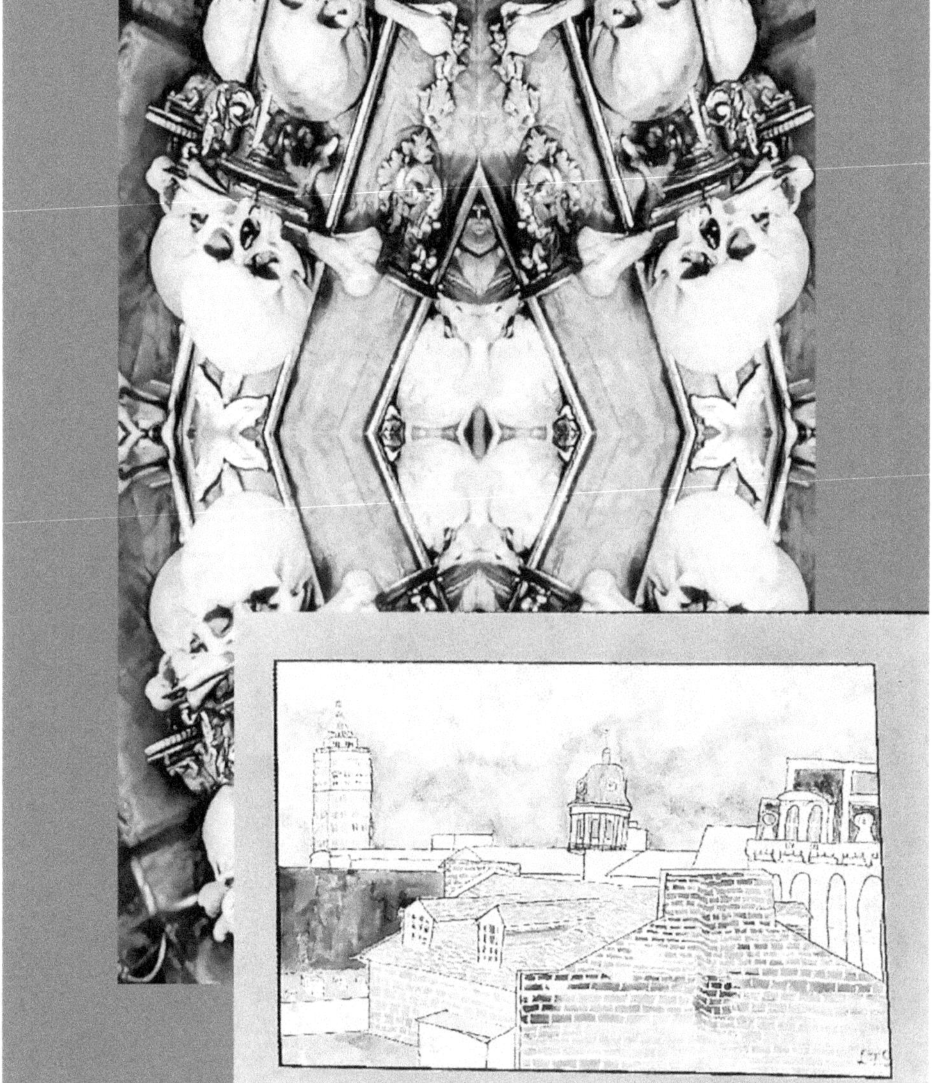

A Living Art

Jehovah's Gift

You entered my life as a shadow
Of a passing cloud; an image
Not of my friend now lost, but
A reflection of what might have been.
Then you were as thin, as intangible,
As a spirit medium's ectoplasm.
Now, in a mere half year, you
Stand beside me, shoulder to shoulder,
Having more strength than Everest.
As I gaze upon your smiling, confident face
I am filled with joy and peace.

MEMory

The Bakery is closed now,
The oven has gone cold.
All the shelves are empty—
Not a crumb remains unsold.

Outside a crowd has gathered
Eager for some more,
But the ling'ring scent of Gingerbread
Is the only thing in store.

The Baker has been called away,
She could not wait for Spring;
She was needed right away
To be the Baker to the King!

Now I am left to carry on
With my store bought Wonder Bread
And Sweet-filled dreams
Of Scrumptious things
As I slumber in my bed.

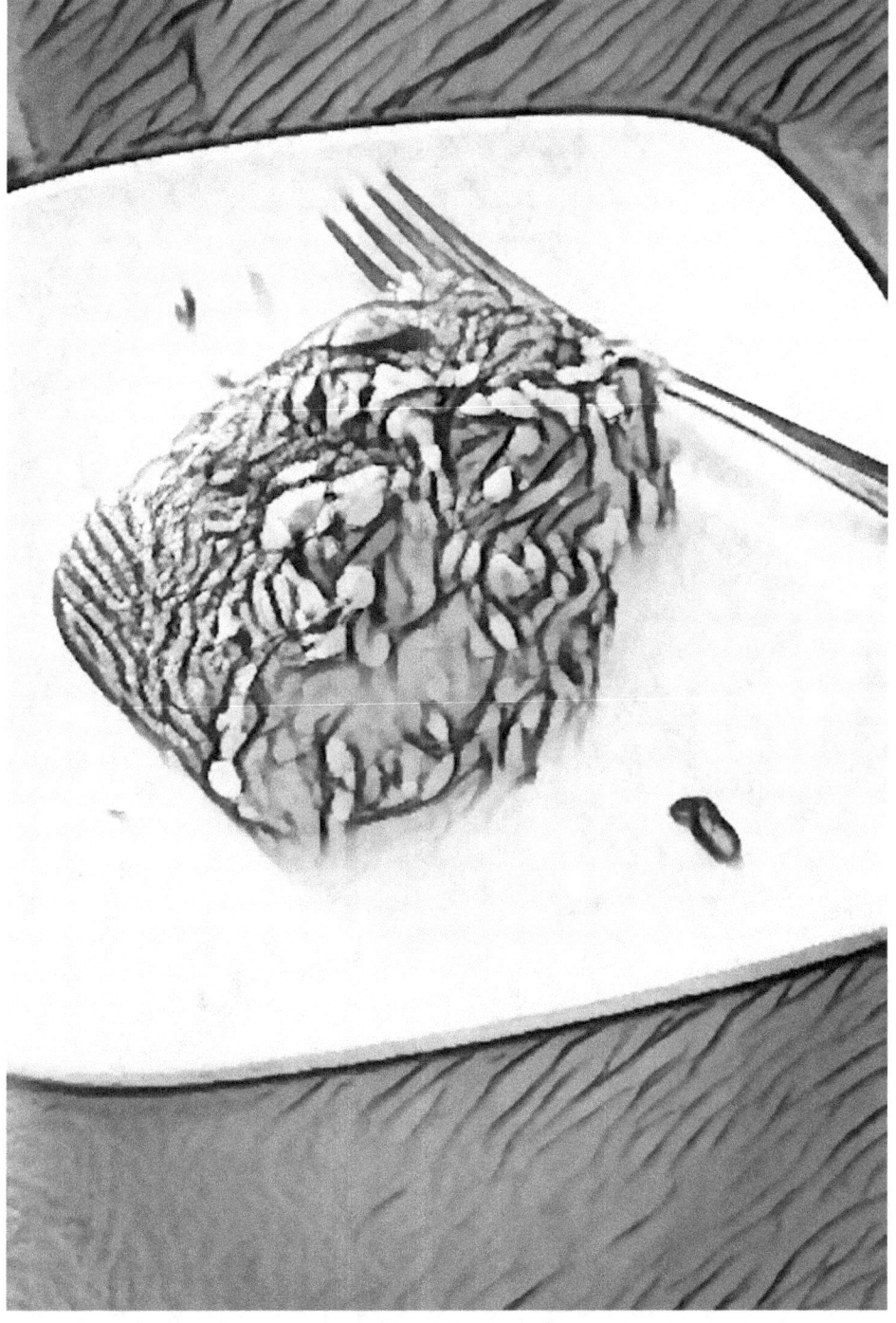

A Living Art

The Torch Bearer

He has spent his life
Bringing light to the dark recesses
And hidden corners of the world.
But the world preferred the darkness.

His eyes have witnessed
Every form of cruelty
And perverse depravity
Man could conceive.
But still he has hope.

Like Stanczyk at Queen Bona's Ball,
He has read the future in a single missive,
Knows that we are all doomed,
And weeps silently, alone,
While those with the power to change Destiny
Danced in oblivion.

He wraps himself in darkness
To hide his wounds—
The thousand cuts and bruises
Left by the uncaring words
Spoken by those he would help.
A lesser man, with thinner skin,
Would have bled out by now.

Still, he carries on.
In place of a Marotte,
He holds a mirror.
In place of jests
And parodies—

A Living Art

Which might bring laughter
And Understanding—
He uses Diogenes blunt words
To challenge people to look at themselves
And see the darkness within.

Few have the courage to listen to his words,
Let alone to gaze into his mirror.
It is easier to mock him,
Shun him,
Push him aside,
And cast him out.
Denied the comfort of human interaction,
He finds solace among the spirits—
The lost souls who learned too late
That he was right.

Historical

Preliterate

Have we lost the skills of the Ancients
To read what cannot be written?
Is there knowledge to be gained from a stone
For those who know how it's bidden?
Though it may sound odd to your ear,
You could read before you knew words:
Ancients could tell food from foe
Just by seeing their tracks and their turds.
A glance at the sun will inform you
The time that is left in the day
The colors of blooms in the forest
Will show it's September or May.
Before we created a language
And Thoth taught to write down its words
We were reading the world and its people
Without need for subjects and verbs.

A Living Art

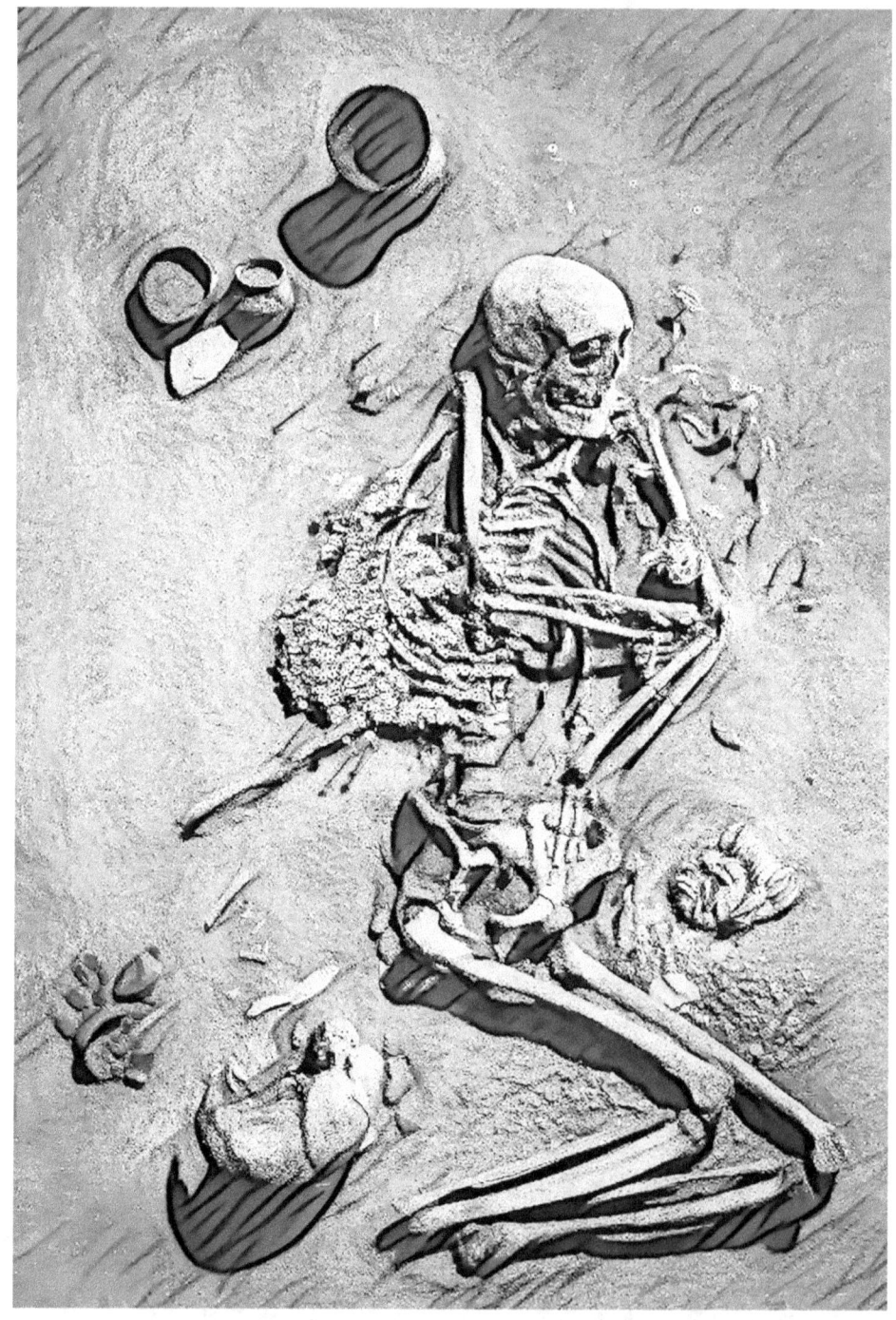

Q

Along the banks of the Vlatava river,
When Khufu ruled in Kemet
And pottery was decorated
With the touch of hempen rope
Men would be buried on their right side
Facing west towards the setting sun.
Women would be buried on their left
Facing east to greet the dawn.
Men would take their knives and axes to the grave
To continue their hunts in the afterlife.
Women would wear their pendants,
And copper earrings—
An egg shaped pot placed at their feet.

But you, you were different.
You didn't fit these narrow definitions
Of Male and Female.
Did you feel like an outsider?
That you didn't have a place in this world?
Was your Father disappointed that you
Weren't a great hunter,
Weren't big and strong,
Preferred softer things?

What role did you play in the tribe?
We, across the void of time,
Will never know.
But of this much we can be certain:
You were brave enough to live
On your own terms,
Defining yourself,

A Living Art

Carving a path in between
Male and Female.
We also know that you were loved
And accepted,
For you were buried on your left
Facing West
With an Egg Pot at your feet.

The Five Burdens

You are the Strong Bull
Whose Birth brings Joy.

You are the One whose laws are Perfect,
Who brings Peace and Tranquility to the Two Lands.
Exalted in the Palace of Amun,
You are Lord of All!

You are He who wears crowns
And pleases the gods!
You are the One who wears
The crown of his Father, Ra!
You are the One who wears the Double Crown
And binds the Two Lands together!

You are the Lord of the Manifestations of Ra!

You are the Living Image of Amun!
Protector of the Sedge and the Bee!
Lord of the Two Lands!
Ruler of Upper Heliopolis!

But you are only eight years old,
And an Orphan.

The Strong Bull is thin and weak,
Limping on his club foot
With the help of canes.

To bring Peace and Tranquility,

A Living Art

You had to abandon your Father's Palace
And Erase all memory of him.

You may wear the crowns,
But they are hollow symbols
Of another's power.
You will never wear the Blue Crown in battle
As your Ancestor Thutmose did,
Racing across the desert in his chariot.
Instead it will be General Horemheb
Who binds the Two Lands in your name,
And wins the Glory.

You are the Lord of the Forms of Ra,
But you cannot change your own.

You are the Living Image of Amun,
But after Seventeen years
Without Sacrifices and Worship,
Amun is Frail and Broken.

For now, you shelter in the shadow
Of Ay, the Vizier,
Biding your time,
And Hoping, one day,
To grow into your names.

In the Valley

The Man in KV-62
Did not survive the crash
His broken leg turned gangrenous-
Though he swore twas just a rash.
It is a shame, he was so young,
At the outset of his life.
A double dose of misery
For his lovely, grieving wife.
It has been months since any sign
Of merriment or mirth
Not even a shadow of a grin
Since her daughter's stillborn birth.
Perhaps that's why he felt the need
To drive out to the marsh—
Sometimes a hunt is just the thing
When life at home's too harsh.
But on the way the axle broke
He was thrown out on the dirt.
Besides the fracture in his leg
It seemed he was unhurt.
Now she is lost, all by herself
Unsure of what to do
While those she loved reside in Peace
In KV-62.

David T. Shoemaker

A Living Art

The Discovery

Near a pile of rubble on the Valley floor
    A straight line—
        An Edge—
           A Step!
Basket by Basket the sand is removed
Leading deeper into the unknown.
And then a Door!
    Intact—
        Sealed—
           Royal!
With hopes high, we send word of our discovery
And refill the hole— to keep out the *other* thieves.
Weeks go by,
The sand is again removed,
The door is opened to reveal:
    Rocks...
        And sand.
More baskets are hauled under the Autumn sun
Until a second door is found.
    Also Intact.
        Also Sealed.
           And with a name:
                Tut-Ankh-Amen!
A small hole is made in the Upper Left Corner.
Beyond the Door—
    Darkness...
        And a void.
We widen the hole.
I insert a candle and peer in:
    First gloom...
        Then Shadows...

A Living Art

Then Forms...
And everywhere the Glint of Gold!

"Can you see anything?"
    I pause, Dumbstruck.
        "Yes. Wonderful things."

Ode to a Grecian Potter

When first Psiax began to paint a terracotta vase
He used his Ebon slurry for body, hair, and face.
With sharpened reed or pointed stick
Fine lines he could incise
To suggest the boy's unruly curls
Or the sparkle in his eyes.
A few more lines define the shape
Of muscles finely toned;
By adding dots of other clays,
The image could be honed.
And yet the image could not be seen
By other's prying gaze
Until Athena set it free
Within the fire's blaze.
Three times the vase must face the heat:
The first to turn it Rust;
Next, to turn it black as night
A hotter kiln's a must.
With vents closed to keep out air
And green wood to make smoke
The clay slip glaze will finally set
To reveal the vase's cloak.

Then one last time with open vents
A lower heat will return
A warm and glowing reddish hue
To the unglazed clay of the urn.
At last the boy has been revealed
With Pan-flute in his hand.
What haunting notes will he invoke
In his mythic sylvan land?

A Living Art

Play on, Sweet Boy! And with your pipes
Many maidens may you charm!
And may Laurel Crowned Apollo
Keep you safe from every harm.

David T. Shoemaker

A Living Art

What Many Have Seen and Heard

If from antiquity to the present,
And since the beginning of Man,
There are men who have seen
The Bodies of Ghosts
And heard the Voices of Spirits,
How can we say that they do not exist?
If none have seen them,
And none have heard them,
Then How can we say they do?
Those who deny the existence of Spirits say:
"Many in the world have heard and seen
Something of Ghosts and Spirits.
But since they vary in Testimony,
Who are to be accepted
As really having heard and seen them?"
Let them hear the tale of Du Bo
And decide.

Long ago, in the Land of Zhou,
When the Xianyun
Attempted to cross the Huai River,
Word came to King Xuan of Zhou
That a woman from the town of Jiangshan
Was secretly betrothed to the Xianyun Prince,
And plotted with him to seize the town.
King Xuan sent his Minister
Du Bo, the Duke of Tengdu,
To the town of Jiangshan
To find and arrest this woman.
Some say Du Bo was beguiled by her Beauty,
Others that she was a witch

A Living Art

Who could change her shape to a cat,
But after a month,
Du Bo returned to the Palace
And told King Xuan that he
Could not find any woman in Jiangshan
Plotting against His Majesty.
King Xuan became enraged,
And ordered his army to Jiangshan
To kill every woman and girl
Within its walls.
Du Bo, in front of the assembled Council,
Admonished the King not to kill the women,
For they were the source of Life
And killing them would kill
The Kingdom in time.
This further enraged King Xuan
Who ordered that Du Bo
Be stripped of his titles,
Bound in Iron,
And Executed at Dawn.
The other Dukes and Lords were shocked
For Du Bo was known for his wise council.

The Royal Auger,
Who could sometimes see
Glimpses of the future,
Came to the King that night.
He told King Xuan that he had seen
Reflected on the surface of the Koi Pond,
Images that foretold the King's fate.
If King Xuan killed Du Bo,
He would never again know peace,
His Kingdom would shatter
Like a dropped porcelain plate,
And he would die a violent death
At the hands of Du Bo's Ghost.
King Xuan laughed.
Believing himself to be All Powerful,

David T. Shoemaker

He dismissed the Auger
And ignored his advice.
In the morning,
Du Bo was killed—
And the King's fate was sealed.
Within a month, the Lords of Tangdu and Jiangshan
Rebelled against King Xuan,
Attacking from the South East,
While the Xianyun pressed in
From the West.

At night, Du Bo came into
King Xuan's Chambers,
And sat mutely at the foot of the bed.
By Day, Du Bo stood in the Shadows
At the South-East corner of the Throne Room.

Month after Month this continued.
King Xuan, unable to find rest
Day or Night
Became Pale and Gaunt—
Almost as Pale and Gaunt
As Du Bo's Spirit.
Illness befell the King
And he was seen less and less frequently
In the courtyards of the Palace.

After three years,
King Xuan was a shadow of his former self
And looked like a man
Twice his age.
His once black locks,
 Were now as White
As Pure Snow
And as Thin and Sparse
As Desert Wheat.
His face was lined
Like crumpled Parchment,

A Living Art

And his hands shook with Palsy.

One night, at a banquet
to honor the engagement of
King Xuan's Son, You Wang
To the Daughter of
The Marquess of Shen,
 King Xuan called out to Du Bo:
"How long must I suffer for my foolishness?
When will my torment end?"
Du Bo replied: "It will end
With your Death."
King Xuan declare: "Then let Death come!"
Du Bo's Ghost emerged from the shadows
Picked up King Xuan's Bow and Arrow
And shot him in the chest.
As the iron point of the arrow
Pierced King Xuan's heart,
A look of relief and peace
Crossed the King's face
And he smiled for the first time
In years.

This was seen and attested to
By all the Lords of Zhou,
As well as their servants,
And the Palace Guards.
All tell the same tale.
Let no one doubt the Truth
Of their words...
...or the existence of Ghosts!

Concerned Citizens

On a cold and windy night
In Nineteen Hundred Three
Sonnichsen and Veness
Boarded Uptown train line C
They would spend the evening slumming
In the Harlem River Club
A Place to Dance,
Play Games of Chance
And Drink whiskey from a tub.

But they were on the job that night,
Not out for fun or sport.
They were there to scope the scene
Before making their report.
They were hired to be the eyes
Of the Committee of Fourteen.
Their accents mask
The secret task:
They move about unseen.

The Committee was convinced
That Modern Life's Upheaval
Was caused by Raines' Law Hotels
And the spreading Social Evil.
So they sent their lowly spies
To Eavesdrop undercover
In ev'ry Dive
And Place to Jive,
Their vices to discover.

The First thing that they noticed

A Living Art

As they entered the Great Hall,
Amid the crush of tables:
The Dance Floor was too small!
But this did not prevent the folks
From gaily joining in
Men danced at ease
Putting their knees
Between their partner's shins!

The dancing was indecent
With its constant Bump and Grind.
White men danced with colored girls
Instead of their own kind.
Men were dancing half undressed,
Girls wore short and skimpy knickers;
And from their mouths
Amid the howls
Came lewd, suggestive snickers.
But worse still were the men in drag,
Those bizarre, effete inverts
Who danced with other dandy fops—
The Flaming Fairy Perverts!
Yet everyone was smiling
And having a grand time.
The Pursuit of Happiness
Shouldn't be a crime!

That doesn't stop Crusaders
With their committees and their spies
From enforcing their morality
While living other lies.
That was a hundred years ago,
We think we've made progress.
But still a man can lose his job
If he prefers to wear a dress.

The Happy Warriors loudly shout
"We must safeguard every child!

A Living Art

No Trans people are allowed
In any room that's tiled!"
"All lives matter", they smugly say
As Black kids die in the street.
"If only they acted more like us,
Their lives would be a treat!"

"The Laws of God must override
The Laws of Man, that's plain."
Tell them that's what ISIS wants,
They'll say "It's not the same!"
It seems there's always Pharisees
To judge how others tread.
I wish they'd show compassion
And empathy instead!

Difficult

They said he was difficult
Because he insisted that he be paid
In cash and in full
Before he would perform.
But they didn't know
How difficult it was
For a black man from the South
To provide for his family
When the White man
Who organized the Show,
Greeted him warmly at the door,
And promised him a place
Among the moon and the stars
Wasn't anywhere to be found
When the show was over.

They said he was difficult
Because he insisted on a rental car
With an Automatic Transmission
And a large trunk
From the time he arrived in the town
Until he returned to the airport
For the next flight.
But they didn't know
How difficult it could be
For a Black Man in the South
To get to the Hotel
Or the Airport
When the promoter leaves
In his car
Without him.

A Living Art

They said he was difficult
Because he demanded
Orange Juice, Snacks, and Sandwiches
In the Dressing Room
And Two Fender Dual Showman Reverb Amps
On the stage. And if—
God forbid!—the promoter
Couldn't get EXACTLY these things
He would impose a fine of $2,000.00
Payable in cash
Before the show.
But they didn't know
How difficult it could be
For a Black Man to find a place
That would serve him food at midnight
Once the show was over.
They didn't realize how hard he worked
To ensure his music sounded
The way his fans expected:
The right way,
His way.
Sure, he could play his music on any amp—
But it would sound more like a cover band
Than his music.

They said he was difficult—
And many other things
I am too polite to repeat—
But they continued to hire him
Month after month
Year after year
Decade after decade
Because 'many people come from miles around
To hear him play his music when the sun go down'.

David T. Shoemaker

A Living Art

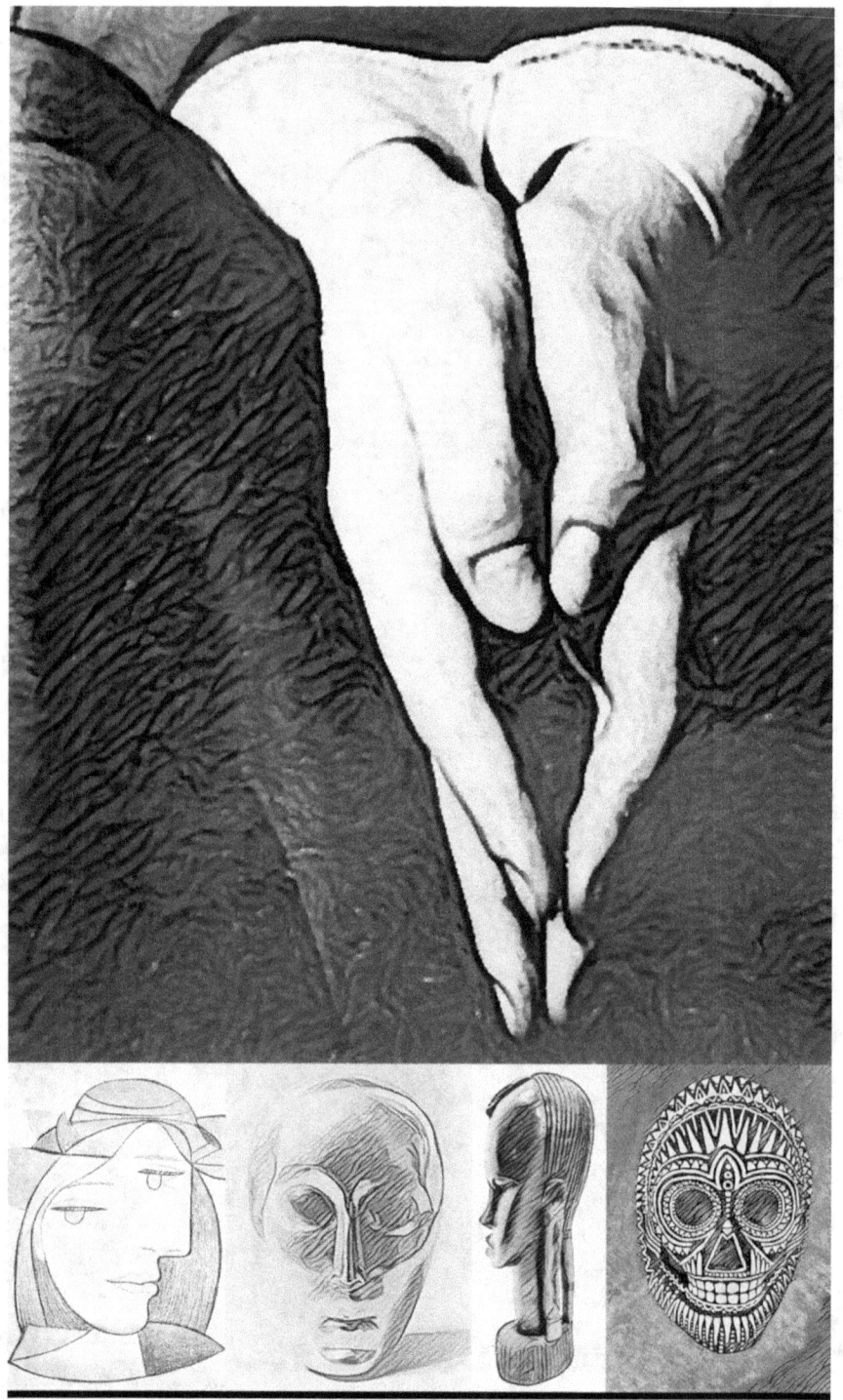

A Living Art

Two friends, Eddie and Charlie
Were sitting in the Golden Swan.
The morning had been given to
This and That, and the afternoon,
Again, had been wasted.
Eddie was eager to make something—
Anything—of his life.
"Let's start a magazine—
A gallery—
A theatre!"
Always a new scheme to become immortal.
In those days, the air was full of new ideas,
New styles of Art,
Of Music,
Of Dance,
Of Architecture.
It seemed every day
A new manifesto was published.
Charlie said, "Let us create a moment."
"What are you trying to say?"
"Remember yesterday, when we went
To the place that is more than a gallery—
Just a place in movement, in transition—
Well, One of the few?"
"Sure. What about it?'
"The walls were emotionally hung
With African carvings,
And there was Yellow, and Orange, and Black.
There were photographs, black and white,
Among them. A photograph of two hands."
Eddie said "Yes, So?"
Charlie replied, "Everything was perfect—

A Living Art

The colors, the light, the image of the hands—
It touched my soul. Time stood still.
That was a moment."
Eddie said, "Moments like that just happen.
You can't make them."
"But what if you could?
What if you dedicated your life
To bringing together the elements
Needed to make moments?
The right clothes,
The right food,
The right friends,
The right...I don't know...
Everything!
You could create a moment!"
"It would take a genius..." Eddie replied.
"But what if you lived your life to create moments,
Used each moment as a brushstroke
On the canvas of your Life.
Your Life would be a Work of Art!"
     "That, my friend, would be a life worth living!"

The Collaborator

Today, the Leader Principle came to my country.
No longer will we have to worry about
Industries leaving our Country,
Foreigners taking our jobs,
Or Religious Minorities corrupting our culture.
Our borders will be secure,
We will stop sending our money overseas,
And we will put our country above all others.
All we have to do is obey the Leader.
No longer will I have to decide
What is the best course of action—
That is the Leader's burden.
I am free to enjoy my new life
As my country restores its Honor
And takes its place as the Greatest Nation on Earth—
As long as I obey.
If the Leader wants me to
Raise my arm
And shout "Hail, My Leader!"
It will not break my arm.
(Not raising my arm in solidarity
 will get it broken for me...)

Prosperity will return for the silent,
While those who speak out,
Who question the wisdom of the Leader,
Will be placed in "protective custody"
............And disappear.
So I will raise my arm,
And add my voice to the chorus,
While inside my troubled heart,

A Living Art

Silently,
I will pray for someone,
Anyone,
To find the courage to resist.
Maybe—someday—that person will be me.
But not today.

HAIL, MY LEADER!

David T. Shoemaker

A Living Art

Demuth's Dove

At Sunnyside Farm in Gap, PA
Wealth mingled with the Artistic Class.
No common leather book to sign—
Guests etch their names on window glass!
Hardware tycoons and business men
May have had a little thrill
From using a glass cutter's tool
Like old John Hancock's Quill.
But such a common workman's tool
Wouldn't suit dear Charlie Demuth.
A grander gesture was required
From an Artist at his zenith.
From his long and slender hand
He removed a diamond ring.
And working, slowly at first,
He made the glass pane sing.
Beneath his name and hallowed date
A Dove of Peace appeared:
Within its beak, a blooming Rose—
A symbol to be revered.
The Guests have all long since gone away
To their eternal rest.
The Heirs have sold the family farm—
But they made a small bequest.
The mural from the cocktail room
And the signed window pane
They gave to the Demuth Museum
Their glory to sustain.

Valentine Conundrum

The Girl:
If of me you sometimes think,
    Return to me this Bow of Pink.
If to me your Heart is True,
    Return to me this Bow of Blue.
If you are another girl's Fellow,
    Return to me this Bow of Yellow.
If to me your Heart is Dead,
    Return to me this Bow of Red.
The Boy:
Pink, Blue, Yellow, Red;
    These are choices that I dread.
How long am I allowed to wait
    Before I tell you of your Fate?
There must be something I can send
    That says I like you as a Friend.
I like the times we sit and Talk,
    And our quiet evening walk.
But you don't make my knees go Wobbly—
    That would be your Brother Bobby!
So I'll send you this bow of Plum
    And hope that you remain my Chum.

David T. Shoemaker

W.W.

It is possible to fly without motors,
But not without Knowledge and Skill;
To step off and soar to the Heavens
From the top of a very steep hill.
In the Air there is quite a sensation
For those brave enough to receive
Of Peace mingled with an Excitement
If that combination you can conceive.
Get rid of the bonds that here bind you
Let go of your burdens and care
Come glide with the Eagles above you
On the Infinite Highway of the Air!

David T. Shoemaker

A Living Art

UVB 76 is a radio station broadcasting a short, monotonous buzz tone repeating at a rate of approximately 25 tones per minute, 24 hours per day. The purpose of the station has not been confirmed by government or broadcast officials. However, the former Minister of Communications and Informatics of the Republic of Lithuania Rimantas Pleikys has written that the purpose of the voice messages is to confirm that operators at receiving stations are alert. Other explanations are that the broadcast is constantly being listened to by military commissariats.

There is speculation published in the Russian Journal of Earth Sciences which describes an observatory measuring changes in the ionosphere by broadcasting a signal at 4625 kHz, the same as the Buzzer.

It is also speculated that the voice messages are some sort of Russian military communications, and that the buzzing sound is merely a "channel marker" used to keep the frequency occupied, thereby making it unattractive for other potential users. The signature sound could be used for tuning to the signal on an old analogue receiver. The modulation is suitable to be detected by an electromechanical frequency detector, similar to a tuning fork. This can be used to activate the squelch on a receiver. Due to the varying emission properties on short-wave bands, using a level-based squelch is unreliable. This also allows a signal loss to be detected, causing an alarm to sound on the receiver.

Another theory, described in a BBC article, states that the tower emits a "Dead Hand" signal that triggers a nuclear retaliatory response if Russia were hit by a nuclear attack. (Source:Wikipedia)

UVB-76, AKA "The Buzzer"

Hnnn.....Hnnn.....Hnnn.....
Twenty five tones a minute
Hnnn.....Hnnn.....Hnnn.....
Twenty four hours a day
Hnnn.....Hnnn.....Hnnn.....
365 days a year
Hnnn.....Hnnn.....Hnnn.....
Since 1973.
Hnnn.....Hnnn.....Hnnn.....
Broadcast by a station that doesn't exist
Hnnn.....Tovarishch.....Hnnn.....
To an audience that doesn't know why
Hnnn.....Hnnn.....Hnnn.....
Some believe it is a dead switch
Hnnn.....Hnnn.....Hnnn.....
That if it ever stops broadcasting
Hnnn.....Hnnn.....Hnnn.....
The missiles will come
Hnnn.....Hnnn.....Hnnn.....
To destroy the enemy
Hnnn.....Hnnn.....Hnnn.....
In their hour of Victory.
Hnnn.....Hnnn.....Hnnn.....
To me, it is
Hnnn.....Hnnn.....Hnnn.....
The heartbeat of the World
Hnnn.....Mir.....Hnnn.....

A Living Art

The Saint

This morning I was born again
A light shined on my face
A Papal hand was pointed
I quickly was embraced.
Out of the darkness I was led
And given a Robe and Crown,
A richly gilded reliquary,
A new name of some renown.

Off I was sent to foreign lands
A new home there to make.
A place to lure the Pilgrim hordes
To revive a dying faith.
So earnestly they come to me
Their favors for to seek:
More crops, more sons, more coins of gold—
The inheritance of the Meek.

But Heaven's Gate to me is barred,
No audience can I gain
To speak with the Eternal Lord
To tell Him of their pain.
My Past is ever present
My Glories not the kind
To win the welcome of a God
With Perfection on His mind.

I've lots of lovely Ladies loved,
And drunk my share of wine.
Oft I held the Thyrsus-Pole
During Eleutherius' time.

A Living Art

I've cheated others to get ahead
And taken the beggar's cent.
But worst of all, for all of this,
I do not repent!

Yet here I sit enthroned above
The Basilica's high altar
Masquerading as a Saint
But the Faithful do not falter.
In their eyes there are no crimes
That cannot be forgiven.
Who am I to cast a doubt
With all that I've been given?

So what if my true name is lost—
I've gained a whole new life!
No longer moldy food for worms
Where blighted rats were rife.
Now I lie encased in glass
For all the world to see.
If not behind the Pearly Gates,
At least down here I'm free!

Sweet Sorrow

On the last day of October
In Eighteen Eighty-Three,
Morning dawned both warm and bright;
Mabel Pruitt shrieked with glee.
Three weeks back she had turned five—
A baby girl no more
She was, at last, old enough
To join the others door to door.
Although their island town was small
A mere six hundred souls
Mabel was determined
To take from all their bowls.
She set off with her brother Jack
Once Father'd cleaned his plate.
The sun still hung low in the sky;
She knocked as people ate.
But she was such a darling
In her gaudy Gypsy clothes
Few neighbors even grumbled
As her treats sweet Mabel chose.
True to her words, she made her rounds,
And went to every house
When treats ov'rflowed her basket
She tucked them in her blouse.
Arriving home at half past eight
Her basket weighed a ton.
She wanted to eat everything,
But her mom just gave her one.
Then she sent her up to bed
After washing face and hands
To slumber snuggly through the night—

A Living Art

Mabel had other plans.
She closed her eyes and feigned asleep
When her folks looked in on her
But once her parents were asleep,
Little Mabel swiftly stirred.
Down the winding wooden stairs
She went softly tread by tread
Pausing only once to check
Her parents stayed in bed.
She took the basket off the shelf
And soon began to eat
It didn't take her very long
To finish every treat!

When dawn broke, her folks came down
And found Mabel on the floor
It looked as if she were asleep,
But she did not stir or snore.
Pa sent Jack to fetch the Doc
But the doctor was too late
There was nothing he could do
To save Mabel from her fate.
So Mother dressed her one last time
And put on her finest dress.
Neighbors filled the front parlor
Their sympathy to express.
Father picked a shady spot
In the yard under the willow.
As they put her in the ground,
A strong wind began to blow.
Late that night, amid the storm
Mother heard a child's screams
And a muffled thudding sound
That kept her from her dreams.

At first light, despite the rain
Pa ran to get his spade
His troubled heart allowed no pause

David T. Shoemaker

Til he unsealed the grave.
It took him just a quarter hour
To move the mounded dirt
His face was streaked with blood red clay
And sweat soaked through his shirt.
With trembling hands he pried the lid
Off the forlorn wooden box.
 What he saw turned instant white
His former sable locks.
Little Mabel lay inside
But she did not lie at rest
She had woken in the night
Trapped in the funeral chest.
She had screamed 'til her lungs bled
And pulled out every hair;
She'd scraped her fingers to the bone
Trying to find air.
Her finger tips were bloody,
There were claw marks on the lid,
But worst of all, he could still see
The tears on her eyelid.
His anguished howls called to his wife,
They fell into a heap;
No one could then imagine
The burden of their grief.
But there was nothing to be done,
Poor Mabel's gone for good.
Pa put the lid back on the box,
Pounding nails into the wood.
Then, slowly now, with heavy heart
He filled the gaping hole
But no balm of Gilead
Could salve the wounds within his soul.

By the time her brother died
In Nineteen Thirty-Six
Sharpley-Schafer had found out
The source that made her sick.

A Living Art

Her body lacked the insulin
To digest and use glucose:
After eating all her treats,
They had found her comatose.
Had they waited long enough—
Perhaps another day—
She might have lived for several years
Instead of dying in the clay.

So if you spend your Halloween
On the Island of Tangier
And head out Trick-or-Treating
You may feel a presence near.
If you see a little girl
Whose hair is all pulled out
Approach to steal your candy,
Do not scream and shout.
It is only little Mabel
Looking out for your welfare—
She doesn't want you in a box
That doesn't let in air!

David T. Shoemaker

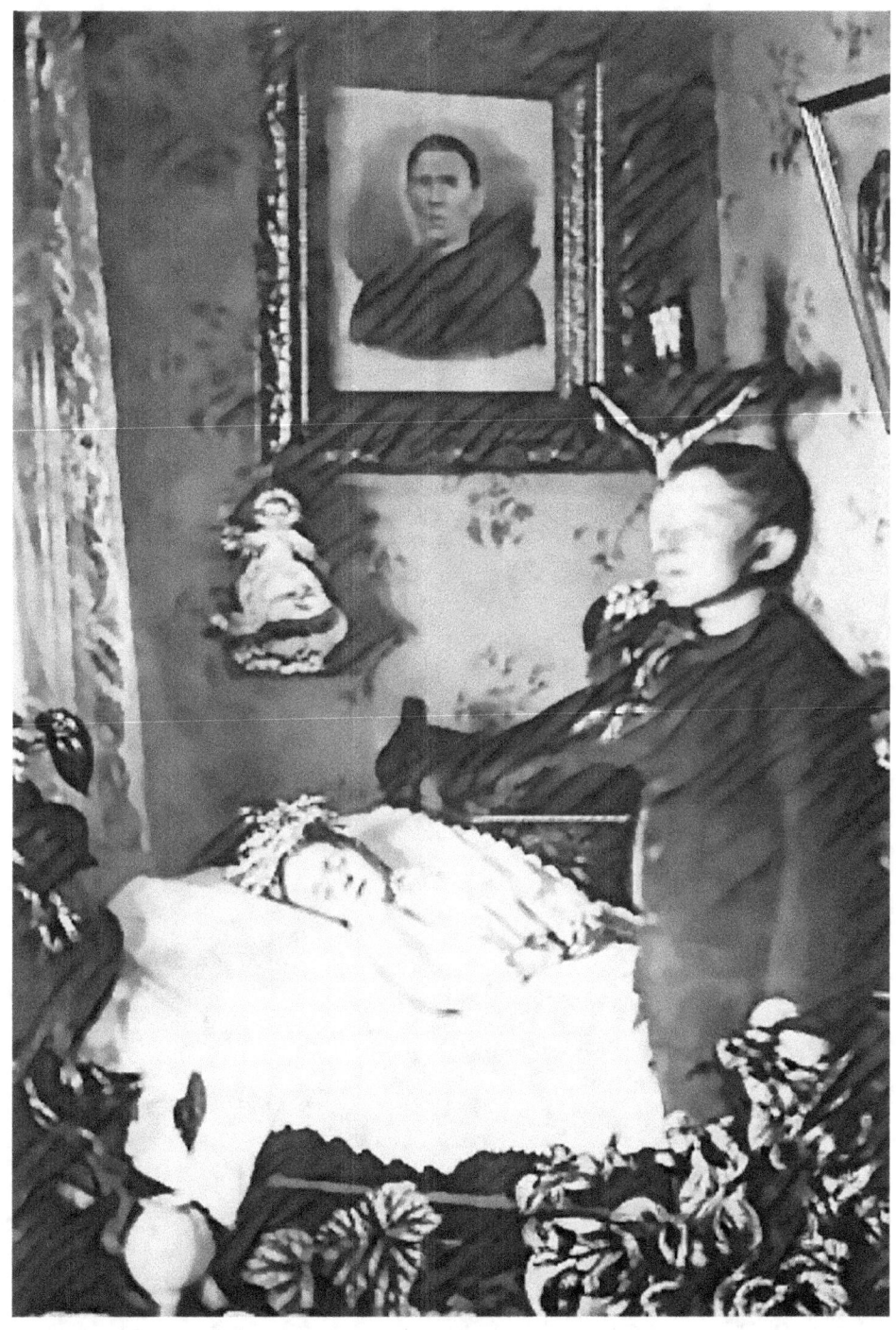

Myth and Folklore

Stingy Jack

Long after Padraig converted the Isle
The Devil would wander in hopes to take back
The souls of the wicked, the cruel and the vile,
And top of the list was the drunk, Stingy Jack!
Jack's heart was as black as Anthracite Coal
His delight the misfortune of others.
In his cups, he'd careen like a newly born foal
And play pranks on his neighbors and brothers.
One night as he staggered his way towards home,
Jack happened to come on Old Nick.
Jack knew he was bound soon to lie in the loam
So he decided to play one last trick.
He begged to be taken to the pub one last time,
To drink of the black stuff his fill.
He drank pint on pint 'til the closing bells chime,
Then announced he'd no coin for the bill.
Jack asked the poor Devil to use his dark powers
To transform himself into a quid.
Once done, Jack declared "We shall keep what is ours"
And the coin in his pocket he slid.
Inside of his pocket, well hidden from view
Was his Mother's old rosary and cross.
It left Lucifer in a terrible stew
For his powers were nothing but dross.
He could not regain his original shape
As long as the cross was so near
Jack told him the only way he could escape
Was to grant him another 10 years.
The Devil was caught in a terrible bind
So quickly he gave his consent.
Jack, to the perils of his soul's future blind

A Living Art

Did not of his cruel ways repent.
Ten years to the day, the Devil came back
To collect the reward once denied.
Jack seeing the Devil enrobed all in black
Went white as a ghost and he cried.
Jack begged for a favor before going away:
"Please let me have something to eat.
An apple from up where the branches do sway
Would be for my gullet a treat!"
The Devil, in kindness, agreed to go up
A big juicy fine one to pick
But once he had reached the branch at the top,
Jack quickly began a new trick.
Around the base of the tree he did spread
A circle of crosses so tight,
That the Devil was trapped with his face glowing red
For he could not descend from his height.

This time Jack was wiser, He asked for much more
Than just one more decade of life:
He demanded if ever he came to Hell's door
He could leave without anger or strife.
The Devil assented, for he knew he was beat
And swore he would ever uphold
If ever again at Hell's door they should meet,
Jack would not get past the Threshold.
Jack lived out his life as ornery as ever
To the ripe age of eighty and eight.
He died in his bed while running a fever
And God met him beside the Pearl Gate.
"Your heart, it is blacker than India Ink
And you've been cruel and spiteful as well.
You've spent all your days in a bottle, I think—
Therefore, I must send you to Hell."
Jack went away sadly and entered the Pit
Where he hoped he'd at least meet a friend.
When he knocked on the door he was met by Old Nick,
Who said that his oath would not bend.

David T. Shoemaker

A Living Art

Jack could not enter the Devil's domain
Nor join with the Angels above;
Instead, he must wander the darkness in vain
Searching for shelter and love.
The sentence was harder than any for Jack,
Who was greatly afraid of the dark.
Jack pleaded with Satan to not turn his back:
"At least give me, Please, just one spark!"
The Devil assented and picked up an ember
Which he gave then to Jack with a grin.
Burning his hand, Jack chanced to remember
A half-eaten turnip, and placed it within.
Jack wanders the night with his lantern held high
In search of a place to call home.
In the fog and the wind, you can still hear him sigh
As the bogs and the valleys he roams.
But if you don't want Jack to enter your home
Where he surely would get into mischief,
Pull a large turnip from out of the loam
And carve out a cypher or glyph.
Or better yet still, carve out a face—
It can be either scary or snide—
Then carve out the middle to create a space
And place a lit candle inside.
Jack will see only a Mara or Daemon
And away from your house he will turn
So make sure the candle is lit every evenin'
To keep away Jack of the Lantern!

Creation

In the Beginning,
There was neither Sun nor Moon,
Snow-Capped Mountain or Fertile Valley,
Solid Ground or Crashing Wave.
There was only Darkness, and the Void,
Whose name was Possibility.
In the Void lived three siblings—
Protos, Oudeteros, and Elektra.
Protos was the Oldest,
Fair of Face and Crowned with Golden Hair.
He was forever telling the others what to do,
Lining them up to do his bidding.
Elektra was the youngest,
An energetic girl with Fiery Red Hair.
She loved to run around,
Skipping and Jumping,
And wandering off unexpectedly.
Oudeteros, the middle child,
Was a stocky boy
With dark hair
And ruddy features.
He was the most passive of the three;
But, also a peacemaker,
Always bringing Protos and Elektra
Back together.
Each of the three had been given
A bag of Magic Marbles.
All of Protos' marbles were Red,
All of Oudeteros' Blue
And Elektra's Yellow.
The marbles were magic

A Living Art

David T. Shoemaker

Because each one contained
Potential.
By themselves,
They were just marbles.
When two of the siblings played together,
Their marbles would bang into each other,
Giving off sparks of light.
This amused the Boys greatly,
And they would often play together,
But Elektra would rather run,
Or Spin, or Dance,
Than play with the Boys.
One day, Elektra noticed
The Sparks flashing in the Darkness
And came running over to see
What it was.
Protos had discovered that,
If they varied the number of marbles
They were playing with,
The color of the sparks would change
From Lilac to Burgundy.
"Ooooh, pretty!" said Elektra,
"Can I play too?"
"Sure! Shoot one of your marbles
Against one of mine!" said Protos.
She did, and an Orange Spark
Flashed in the dark.
"Now shoot one at Oudeteros' Marble!"
A green spark flared and faded.
"OK, Everyone shoot one at the same time!"
Shouted Protos.
When the three marbles crashed together,
There was a large 'Bang!',
And the first Hydrogen Atom was born.
This was the beginning of the Beginning,
But there was still just the Void,
And the Children,
And Hydrogen.

A Living Art

Over time, the Three learned that
Using two marbles each produced Helium,
And the more marbles they used,
The heavier the elements created.
Eventually, they used all the marbles
In their bags, and Every Element was born.

Rustam's Fire

There are many tales in the Shahnameh
Of Rustam of Zabulistan,
The Marzban of Sistan,
Hero of Persia.
Most tell of a Mighty Warrior—
Killer of the Mad Elephant of Manuchehr,
Conqueror of the Impenetrable Fortress on Mt. Sipand,
Destroyer of the White Demon Div-e Sefid.
But despite all of the slaughter,
Rustam was a humble man,
Content with simple things.
It was this simplicity, they say,
That brought into being a companion,
A protector from disease,
And a defender of the Grain.
I speak, of course, of the Cat.

One day as Rustam was out
Riding among the almond
And pistachio groves
He heard a cry for help
Echoing across the rocky valley.
He spurred his horse on,
And found an old man,
Beaten, bleeding, and recently robbed.
Rustam tore the hem of his robe
To bandage the old man's wounds.
Then Rustam helped him into the saddle
 Of his own mighty steed.
Walking beside his horse,
Led him to his camp.

A Living Art

There he lay the old man on his bedroll
Gave watered wine to revive him,
And coaxed him back from the edge of Ersetu.

When he was sure the old man would recover,
Rustam left his tent to find food.
He killed a goat on the mountainside
And brought it back to camp with wild herbs.
He roasted it over the fire outside the tent
As Shamash drove his chariot
Home to E-Babbarra.
The aroma from the campfire
Drew the old man from the tent.
Sitting beside Rustam, the old man
Thanked him for saving his life
And asked what gift he could bestow
To repay his Life-Debt to Rustam.

Rustam smiled wistfully,
And shaking his head, replied:
"I already have everything
A man could wish for:
The warmth and comfort of the fire,
The scent of the smoke,
And the beauty of the stars overhead."

The old man nodded, deep in thought.
Suddenly, the old man stood up
And reached into the fire.
He pulled out a handful of smoke
And a single flickering flame.
He began to slowly knead them,
Gently giving them a new form.
After a few minutes, the Mage
(for he truly was a powerful Wizard)
Drew down the two brightest stars
And pushed them into the ball of smoke.
He continued to knead and shape the ball,

David T. Shoemaker

A Living Art

Occasionally drawing out a spindly thread of smoke,
While Rustam watched in amazement.
At last, the old mage spoke:
"In a short time, this fire will die,
The smoke will blow away,
And the Dawn will erase the stars.
Please accept this embodiment
Of the pleasures you treasure
With my eternal gratitude."

Into Rustam's lap, the mage set
A small grey kitten, with fur like smoke,
A small red tongue that darted like a flame,
And two blue eyes, as bright as stars.
The cat settled into Rustam's lap
Sharing its warmth,
Purring softly, like a crackling fire.
Thus the first Persian Cat was born,
And Rustam was greatly pleased.

The Wedding Guest

Long ago, in Napoli
A maiden was seduced
And though she loved the boy a lot
She felt she'd been reduced.
She feared that having had his fun
The boy would run away.
So she went to Fontanelle
In the cavern crypt she prayed.
She asked the Captain for his help
To make the boy her groom.
But while her head was deeply bowed,
The boy came in the room.
He laughed at her naivety
Then turned to the Captain's skull
"You have no power, you lump of bone!
You're nothing but a cull!"
Then sticking his knife in the skull's left eye
The boy loudly professed
"If ever we are joined as one,
You shall be my guest!"
Seasons came and seasons went
And the boy forgot his boast.
But silently at night he heard
The prompting of the ghost.
No matter how often he would stray
His thoughts always returned
To the beautiful young maid
That he so cruelly spurned.
The Captain guided every dream
Back to her loving face.
He banished thoughts of other girls,

A Living Art

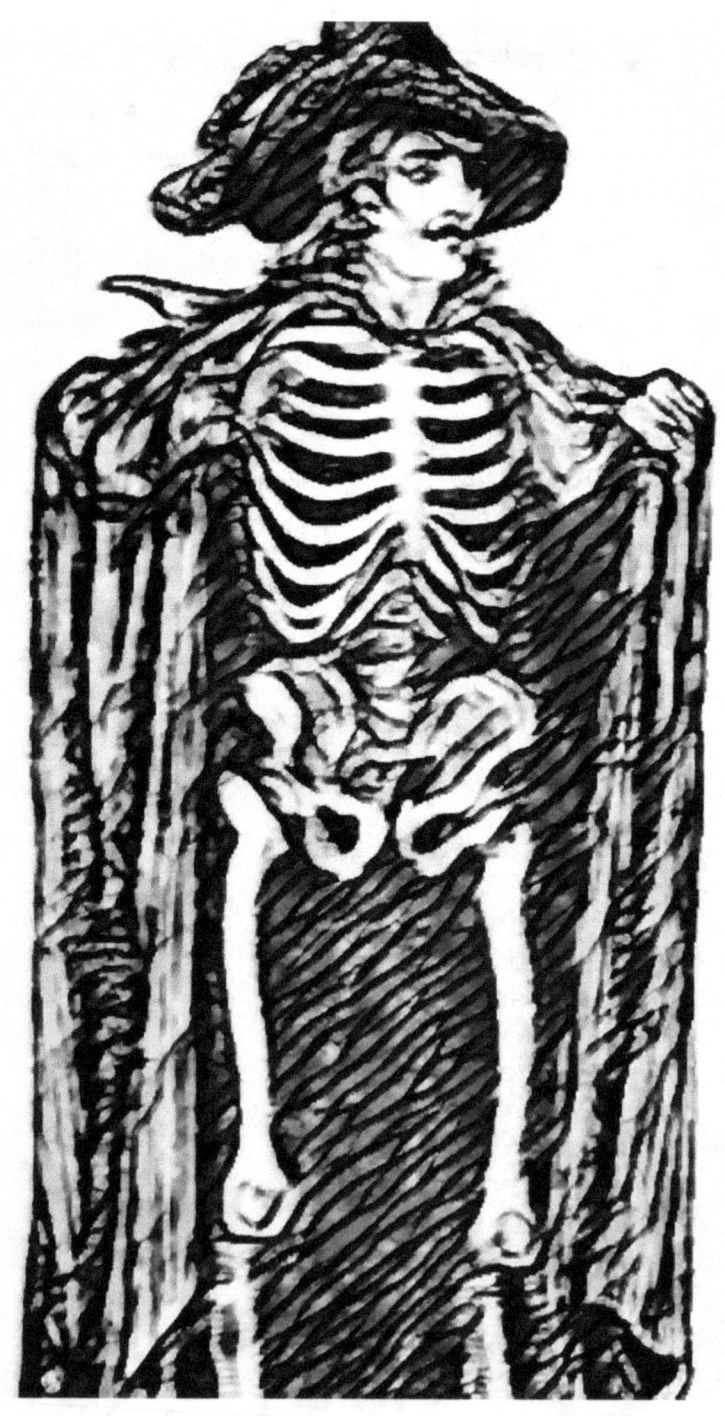

David T. Shoemaker

Their features he'd erase.
Til at last the boy gave in
And asked her for her hand.
Within a month he sealed his vow
With a golden band.
That night a lavish feast was held
To which the town came out.
Around the edges of the crowd,
A stranger lurked about.
He wore clothes that were out of style,
An ancient soldier's suit
With silver braid on each shoulder
And a cavalryman's boot.
Across his face he wore a patch
To cover his left eye.
A satisfied grin would cross his face
Each time he saw the bride.
A jealous rage consumed the groom
When he saw the soldier's smile.
He roughly grabbed the older man
And dragged him to the aisle.
"Who are you to join this feast?
Who gave you an invite?"
"You did." Said the older man
"In the Fontanelle at night."
The groom's face turned deathly pale,
His knees to gelatin.
As proof, the Captain undid his coat
To reveal a skeleton.
"Be kind to her, and ever true."
Said the Captain through his beard.
"Remember, I am watching you."
He turned, and disappeared.

A Living Art

The Refugee Child

The refugee child remembers
Being dragged from his bed
In the middle of the night
By his father.
The look of terror on his mother's face
As she covers his mouth
To stifle his crying.

The refugee child remembers
Hiding in the shadows
As the death squads
March through his town.

The refugee child remembers
The smell of donkeys and camels
And the unusual spices in the marketplace.
The sound of foreign languages—
Sometimes harsh, sometimes soothing—
Which he could not understand.

The refugee child remembers
The kindness of strangers—
Usually the poor or downtrodden—
Who would smile at him
And sing and dance
And share what little food they had.

The refugee child remembers
The suspicious looks he received
From the guards in the plaza,
The looks of disgust and loathing

A Living Art

From the wealthy elite
Who saw him—not as a child in need—
But as a drain on the economy.

The refugee child remembers
Arriving back home
Once the conflict was over
To discover he was the only child left.

The refugee child remembers
The anguish and guilt he felt
For surviving when so many others had died.
The loneliness, the isolation,
The responsibility to be worthy.

The refugee child knows what is important
And what is fake;
Whom to trust, and whom to avoid;
What to keep, and what to cast away.

The refugee child is Jesus the Christ
Appointed by God
To judge all people
Because the refugee child remembers.

A Visit from Krampus

December 5th is Krampusnacht!
All children should take care
For the Horned Goat Devil is on the prowl
To punish Evil everywhere.
His long black fur conceals his chains
But you can hear his chiming bell.
Upon his back a deep basket
To haul bad children off to Hell.
Between his fangs, a long red tongue
Dangles past his chin and chest:
One quick lick is all he needs
To perform his little test.
If you taste sweet, he'll let you be
And tell St. Nick you deserve a gift;
But if he detects a sour note
Your punishment will be swift!
He will use his chain to bind you tight
Then grab his birch rods in his fist.
He will thrash you to drive the evil out
He lets no rottenness persist.
A second lick decides your fate:
Are you rancid or are you sweet?
The sweet will earn kind Santa's gift
The rest, the Devil gets to meet.
So if you are out on Krampusnacht,
Remember to say your prayers!
Confess your sins before bed each night
So you are not caught unawares.
Krampus delights in his new role
As the punisher of the vile.
His chains are heavy and chafe a lot;

A Living Art

His beatings are not mild.
If you are bad, you have more to fear
Than a mere lump of coal in your stocking—
The Lake of Fire could be your fate
When Krampus comes a knocking!

David T. Shoemaker

A Living Art

The Galleon

Oh, to bear the burden of this curse
Spoken aloud, with crystal skull in hand,
That those who raid the Incan Temple's purse
Should never again find peace or rest on land.
Warned we were to never touch the gold
Or we would be a heathen demon's slave
We mocked the curse, pretended to be bold
Certain to find home's shore or watery grave.
But true it was, and we are doubly damned:
Each man of us aboard this ghostly ship—
From keel to deck with gold and jewels jammed—
Would give it all to find a welcome slip.
For though we would be richer than a king
No joyful slumber will it ever bring.

Seasons

Nature

How do we learn to see Nature?
To see the Forest
When all around are trees?
Spring comes to the backyard
With the same signs and wonders
As the fields and meadows—
The redness of new leaves opening stickily,
The spikes of the crocus,
The songs of the Robins and Peepers.
Day by day,
The Sun rises earlier
And sets later;
But we say that's Daylight Savings Time.
The Supermarkets are full
Of hothouse fruits and vegetables
That used to be the eagerly awaited gifts
Of the changing seasons.
Still, Nature persists.
She reveals herself in a thousand quiet ways,
Reminding us that the Earth is our home
And our Mother.
She nurtures and feeds us,
But she needs to be protected
From those who would rape and pillage her.
Every day, she speaks to us,
Revealing her beauty and her fragility
To those who slow down enough to listen.

Januarius

The Wolves of Winter gather
As Janus guards the Gate.
The Two-Faced God can see both ways
To foretell about your Fate.
He was there before the World
Guarding Heaven's Door;
He divided the cosmic Void
And created the first Shore.
He is the God of Beginnings—
Here's a secret seldom told:
Every moment is a beginning,
By him, all Fates controlled.
We like to think that every deed
Has a start, a middle, an end.
In truth, there's just the Start of Next;
Thus Fate Janus can wend.
He does not crave attention
Like Jupiter or Mars,
But he sees more than both combined
And is the Master of the Stars.
So if you are in trouble,
Begin all of your prayers
By asking for kind Janus' help
To alleviate your cares.
He will look into your past
To see where you went wrong;
Then looking forward, seek a Path
To guide your life along.
Sing Janus' praise this New Year's Day
As we begin a new transition
And ask his help with each new task
To bring them to fruition.

David T. Shoemaker

A Living Art

Spring

Do not be an April Fool!
It was not always Spring—
Or Spring-Time, or Springing Time—
For a Courting Couple's Fling.
We did not always speak of things
Like the Springing of the Leaf,
Or Spring of Day and Spring of Moon
Upon the High Lord's Fief.
Even Noble Chaucer chose to
Speak of April's Showers
That soak the thirsty earth of March
Instead of Springing flowers!
Before we spoke of Bud and Bloom
We called the Season Lencten.
It marked the end of Gloom and Dark
When the days began to lengthen.
But now that word has largely gone,
Who knows wherefore it went?
It lingers dimly in the Church
As the fasting time of Lent.

Come Away

Today, my Love, the south wind blows
All laden with warmth and treasure.
Come away, come away to the open fields
And bask in this glorious weather!

Robins and wrens are filling the air
With the music of Courtship and Love.
Come away, come away to the wildflower glade
And attend to the concert above!

The snows have all melted from the mountains and fields
To the delight of the beavers and otters.
Come away, come away to the Brandywine Creek
And wade in its crystalline waters!

My heart is astir with the first touch of Spring
And I would we were happy together.
Come away, come away where the brown woods breathe
And the green creeps over the meadow!

Away from the soot and the grime of the city
With its clamorous noises and strife
To the peace and the calm of this beautiful valley
For renewal of Love and of Life!

© Alison Hartpence and David T. Shoemaker

David T. Shoemaker

Mother's Night

It started with the harvest,
This ever creeping gloom.
The greens of Summer fade away,
Trees blaze orange and maroon.
The days grow ever shorter,
The year heads to its tomb.
Some fear that this may be the end;
But hope grows in Frigga's womb.
Calmly she sits at her spindle,
Spinning the threads of Life
While within her the new year sleeps
Awaiting the midwife.
Snows fall to spread a blanket
Across the slumbering earth.
Shepherds hurple in the cold
Eager for the child's birth.
With flaming brand light torchieres,
In fields, build bonfires high!
On each hearth may a Yule Log blaze,
Let Carols reach the sky!
Tonight is born the Lord of Light,
Let every household cheer!
May Peace envelope every heart
As we greet the newborn year.

David T. Shoemaker

Melancholia

Voices from the Abyss

I hide the torment of my heart behind a smiling face
The side of me that wants no part of this eternal race.
I hear the voices in my head, those ever-present foes
Denounce the life that I have lead as the source of other's woes.
They twist the truth inside my brain like an ever-swinging noose
Until it seems each friend I gain I will just as quickly lose.
For who would choose to stand by me in the hour of my pain?
The crush of my insanity leaves me alone again.
The e-mails that I've sent remain unanswered day by day;
"You're the source of all their pain" my inner voices say
"They'd rather let the friendship die than put up with your grief".
Yet still I hope for your reply, no matter if it's brief.
A quick kind word is all I need to gain the strength to fight;
Without it every doubt will feed on the silence brought by night.
Each passing hour from the Ghost's High Noon 'til the blood red of the dawn.
Would be as silent as the tomb but for the whispered song
Repeated without end inside my deeply troubled mind
"They would have, by now, surely replied if you were worth their time".
I remember all the laughs we've shared, and I smile at your name
And hope as much as I have cared, you'll care for me the same.

A Living Art

I know this much of friendship, it's frightening but it's true
You can give your love to someone else, but it may not return to you.

David T. Shoemaker

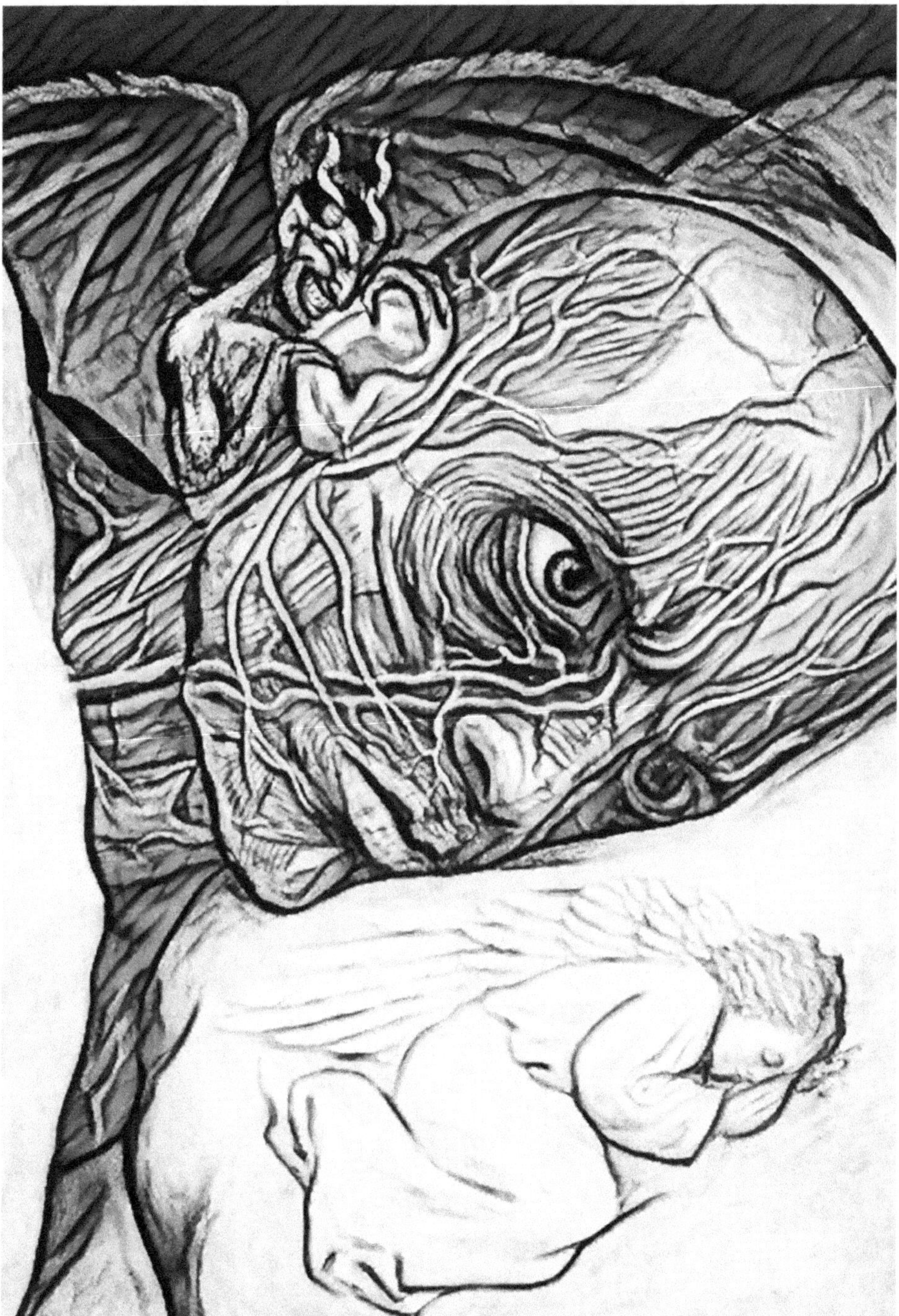

A Living Art

Lebensmüde

It takes so much energy to be cheerful,
To force yourself to smile
When inside
Every fiber of your being
Is an empty husk.
When the light leaves your eyes
Like a dying flashlight.
When your laughter becomes the echo
Of a lone person
Walking through a vacant house.
Still, you put on the mask
To reassure friends and family
That everything is ok.
To hide the pain.
To be normal.
But day by day
The battery grows weaker.
An eternity of slumber
Is a temptation
That is hard to resist.

3 a.m.

I lie awake and wonder
why my Heart no peace can find
Why it takes the certainties of life
and twists it in my mind
Like a noose.

High upon life's gallows I stand
surveying all the land that round me lies.
I see the foolishness of those who claim it
Only to lose it when they die.

If I live it is only because of you
I was dead before I met you
Without you I'll just return to the grave.

The Life which has been given is too easily lost
I need the reassurance of your smile

Will no one save me?

The Last Goodbye

Heartbeats echo through my empty soul
Like footsteps in a fog strangled alley
Now that you are gone.
Each day dawns in a darkness
Unbroken by the sun;
The shadow of our friendship
Has created a permanent eclipse,
Blocking out all joy.

I wonder if you also live within its shadow
Or if you have escaped to the blissful shore
Of a new life; a life without me.
I hope you have, for I would not wish
This desolation on anyone.

I cannot take a step without passing
A memento of the better times we shared:
Of knowing laughs,
Shared confidences,
And struggles met and conquered
Side by side.
Even the hours spent sitting together
In the parking lot outside your home,
An ending to an evening we didn't want to end.

Did you realize how much a part of my life
You had become? Did I do enough
To prove to you your worth?
Or did I, as I suspect
Take without giving?
You deserve so much more
Than I can give.

A Living Art

And now the damage has been done
The vessel shattered
Its treasure lost forever.
The only solace I can find
Is the cold embrace of the grave.

Please forgive me.

David T. Shoemaker

A Living Art

Bardsong

The time has come to beat the muffled drum
To call the clan together.
I must put on the mantle of a bard
And sing stories of my fallen father's greatness.
It is a duty I was born to bear—
A shadow looming across my path
For a score of years,
Since my Father sang the Lifesong for his Dad.
Now it is my turn to give him one last gift,
To form in the fog of one's mind
A living being.
It must be a song so sweet and strong
To knit a body for the afterlife;
There must be magic in the song to hold the soul,
Powerful images to make him real,
Once the substance of his life
Dissolves into dust.
Therefore, I must set aside my shattered heart,
And the silent, shadowed emptiness I feel
And sing him back to life.

Identity

When I look into a mirror
Whose face do I see?
It is not my own,
Though it is close—
Distorted,
Reversed,
Opposite of me.

When I read the things I wrote
When I was young and foolish,
Do I see me
Or someone else
I used to be?

Is there something real,
Something permanent,
That defines who I am?
It is not height or weight,
Nor the color of my hair.
Facial Recognition Software might compare
The Size, Shape, and Position
Of my Eyes, Cheeks, Nose, and Jaw
To find me in a crowd.

But how do I find myself
When I am adrift upon a sea
Of memories and sensory information?
Constantly shifting and updating,
Erasing the Past to make room for the Future—
Who am I really?

David T. Shoemaker

Advice

A Caesaries

Do not run away and hide
Or let your face turn red
If people call you "Little Boots"
Or lack hairs upon your head.
These little, taunting words are meant
To bring the mighty low;
Spoken by those whose lives do not
Have victories to show.
Embrace the name, and live your life
Secure in who you are—
Then watch the taunter's eyes grow big
As you dance among the stars!

Lessons from Master Fong

Do not meet strength with strength:
Someone is always stronger.
Do not push back when you are pushed:
Redirect your opponent's energy
To take him to the floor.

Find the energy within you
And then center it:
Move from the left and from the right
Into the center
There none can take you.

Relax and enjoy life
When you are tense
You are easily pushed
And will feel every blow.
Stay loose and flow instead!

David T. Shoemaker

A Living Art

Uncle Peter's Philosophy

A day off is a day a man takes for himself,
A day without structure or aim;
A break from the grind of his daily routine—
A day in pursuit of things other than fame.

We matriculate at birth this School of Life
And graduate on the day that we die
And the days in between are a checklist of goals
As we struggle and fight to scrape by.

It's important to note that there's more than one path
As we wander our way through the grime,
And it's healthy to stop and set down our pack
To steal a confection of Time!

Friendship

Forever seems, at times, too long to hope for
Relationships between two friends to last
In this world, this life, and yet
Even this is
Not impossible with love.
Devotion and commitment
Spring up from our
Hearts, bringing life, and
Insuring that, as friends, no
Pain is too great to bear.

Karma

I stand on the shoulders
Of Everyone and Everything
That's come before:
Grandparents,
    Parents,
        Teachers,
           Friends,
The many Quaint and Curious Volumes of forgotten lore.
All Lift me up,
    Let me see further,
        Bring me closer to God.

I stand Tall and Proud,
Unbowed and Unbent
By the burden of all those I carry on my shoulders:
Coworkers,
    Neighbors,
        Companions,
           Lovers,
The Stranger on the street corner hustling for a buck,
Cast away by Society.
With the words I speak,
    The food I share,
        The door I hold open,
           Or just a Smile,
I lift up those around me.

I am in the middle
Of a Great Chain of Humanity,
Forever Lifting and being Lifted,
But I am Blind to the infinite threads of Life

A Living Art

That bind us together.
I may feel the feet upon my shoulders,
Or the strength of the one who holds me,
Without ever knowing whom they lift,
Or by whom they are lifted.
Still, we are all connected—
Lifting or Lifted—
We become one.

David T. Shoemaker

Saying Goodbye to Honalee

When I was young, I used to dream
Of Pirate maps and daring schemes,
Relics buried in the sand
And roaming distant, foreign lands,
Sailing on a square-rigged brig
Or dancing Dublin's Irish jig,
Being knighted by the Queen,
Or serving as a college Dean.
But in all of these I was alone,
For you were yet to me unknown.

When I met you, my dreams were changed,
Priorities were rearranged.
To make you smile became my goal,
All your tears I would console.
In place of Palladian Estate
A simple cottage by a lake.
By the fireside we would sit,
I would read and you could knit.
I would cook and you would teach
Our kids about the QB sneaks.
Our lives might seem ordinary,
Unlike tales of Myth or Fairy,
But you have brought me greater joy
Than any dream of a young boy.

David T. Shoemaker

About the Author

David T. Shoemaker describes himself as a Poet, Artist, Philomath, and Endomorph. He was first exposed to the craft of writing poetry in a 5th Grade Poetry Workshop for advanced English students. He has been called an "Historian Poet" for his tendency to weave history, archaeology, and folklore into bardic verse. His poems are included in the "Timeless Voices" (2006) and "Forever Spoken" (2007) anthologies edited by Howard Ely. In 2017, he released the CD "Bardsongs" which featured him reading his poetry.

He is currently working on developing a series of walking tours in Lancaster PA based on the life and works of Charles Demuth, an early 20th century American artist who helped introduce modernist principles to American Art, founded the Precisionist Movement, and influenced such diverse artists as Georgia O'Keeffe, Jasper Johns, Andy Warhol, and Robert Indiana.